an

v:

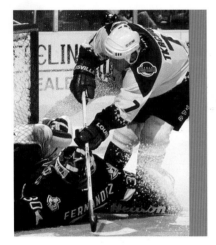  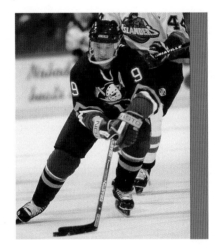

HOCKEY THE NHL WAY
Goal Scoring

Sean Rossiter

GREYSTONE BOOKS
Douglas & McIntyre
Vancouver/Toronto

For Rocket Richard, who scored 626 goals, most of them playing his off-wing.

Greystone Books
A division of Douglas & McIntyre Ltd.
1615 Venables Street
Vancouver, British Columbia
Canada V5L 2H1

Canadian Cataloguing in Publication Data
Rossiter, Sean, 1946 –
    Hockey, the NHL way: goal scoring

    ISBN 1-55054-550-7

    1. Hockey—Juvenile literature. I. Title.
GV848.7.R68 1997   j796.962'2   C97-910321-5

Editing by Anne Rose, Kerry Banks
Cover and text design by Peter Cocking
Front cover photograph: *Sergei Fedorov* by Tony Biegun/Bruce Bennett Studios
Instructional photographs: Stefan Schulhof/Schulhof Photography
Back cover photographs by Bruce Bennett Studios. Photographers:
    Keith Tkachuk, Paul Kariya, Mark Messier: Bruce Bennett •
    Jaromir Jagr: Richard Lewis • *Joe Sakic, Tony Amonte:* John Giamundo
Printed and bound in Canada by Friesens
Printed on acid-free paper

Every reasonable care has been taken to trace the ownership of copyrighted visual material. Information that will enable the publisher to rectify any reference or credit is welcome.

The publisher gratefully acknowledges the assistance of the Canada Council for the Arts and of the British Columbia Ministry of Tourism, Small Business and Culture.

Contents

The NHL Way team

Our players

Jordan Sengara

Daniel Birch

Will Harvey

Tyler Dietrich

Michelle Marsz

Rob Tokawa

Brandon Hart

Kendall Trout

Jesse Birch

Nicolas Fung

Brian Melnyk

Scott Tupper

Special thanks

Special thanks, first, to the parents of the NHL Way All-Stars; your sons and daughters reflect your love and dedication. Thanks also to David McConnachie, director of publishing for the NHL; to Chris Brumwell and Devin Smith of the Vancouver Canucks; to Rick Noonan and the staff at the UBC Thunderbird Winter Sports Centre; and to Mike Harling of Sportsbook Plus, who provided research materials and helpful advice. Todd Ewen of the San Jose Sharks is, as always, a valued friend of this project.

Our coaching advisory staff

Paul Carson
Coach coordinator, the British Columbia Amateur Hockey Association

An assistant coach of the UBC Thunderbirds, Paul Carson is also the provincial coach coordinator responsible for coach development programs in B.C. He is a master course conductor for the NCCP, and coached high school hockey in Sendai, Japan. He recently completed work on the CHA Hockey Curriculum series.

Bill Holowaty
Minor hockey coach

Still the third-highest scorer in UBC Thunderbird history, Bill Holowaty played and coached professionally and worked as a hockey school instructor in Japan for seven years. He played for Canada's gold-medal team at the World University Games in 1982, and on Canada's first Spengler Cup winners of 1985.

Ken Melnyk
Author, the Hockey Skills Development Program, Tykes/Atoms

Named coach of the year (1995–96) by the B.C. Amateur Hockey Association, Ken Melnyk was on the organizing committee for the 1988 Winter Olympics. He wrote the Games' deficit-free business plan. However, Ken's most notable achievement may be Brian Melnyk, one of our NHL Way players.

Jack Cummings
Hockey coordinator, the Hollyburn Country Club

Jack Cummings played goal for four years at both the Junior A level and with the University of Alberta. He was an assistant coach to the U of A's legendary Clare Drake for six years, and has been hockey coordinator at the Hollyburn Country Club in West Vancouver for four years.

"One-timing the puck is a good way to score. Have your legs shoulder-width apart. Grip your stick firmly. Keep your eyes on the puck right to your stick. Practise it standing and moving."

WAYNE GRETZKY

Foreword

Scoring goals is the most fun you can have playing hockey. Maybe you think that the ability to score is something you're either born with—or without. Maybe you think that goal scorers simply have a mysterious gift.

Scoring goals is not magic. You can *learn* what to look for and how to react. What is the goalie doing, and what should you do when you see the netminder move? Where should you shoot the puck to have the best chance to score? When should you shoot? When should you deke? This book answers all those questions.

Scoring goals is a numbers game. The numbers are not the totals of goals and assists you collect. The numbers are the options you see as each scoring chance develops.

With this book, you can learn what the best option is in any situation. If you see it won't work, move on to the next option. There is always more than one way to score.

This book puts you one-on-one, face-to-face with the goalie. These are the most exciting plays in hockey. And when you have the puck, you have the edge.

Brian Burke
Senior vice-president and director of hockey operations
NHL Enterprises

Introduction

Goal scorers don't get enough credit.

Oh? It's the goal scorers who get the big bucks, right?

Some coaches think all goal scorers do is tap some gift—a gift they were born with. Some people think goal scorers can do only one thing: score goals.

Here's a little secret. Goal scorers understand the game of hockey from the inside out.

Look for yourself. Goal scorers don't follow the puck; they know where the puck is going. They are the players whose sticks the puck seems to find. A goal scorer sees the game differently.

In this book, we have broken down scoring opportunities into choices, to show you how it's done—like a slow-motion video replay. But a goal scorer moving to the net already knows whether the goalie is in or out, and where the goalie's catching mitt is. The puck is already in the net. A goal scorer sees more, knows more, is more aware. The moves are automatic.

So learn everything you can. Learn every time you step onto the ice. Whether it's a practice or a game or just street hockey on rollerblades, work on something. Perfect a move. Fool around with your stick. Try something you've never done before. Learn about goaltending. Most of all, watch closely. Be a student of the game.

Take that attitude into the game. Take everything in. Know the situation: How many minutes left? How do they play? Who's your check? Is this a delayed penalty? Take a look. Be in the game.

Because that's how to enjoy hockey—by learning more of its secrets. Scoring goals isn't why you play hockey. It's the voyage, not the destination that counts. Goals are the icing on the cake.

"The key is getting your shot off as quickly as possible. If you wind up, it gives the goalie more time to react. The quicker your shot is, the tougher it will be for the goalie to stop it."

KEITH TKACHUK

If you want to be a goal scorer, you have to shoot the puck. You know that already. But you often see a player in a great scoring position—in the slot, for example—passing the puck. Why? Because that player doesn't want to be the one who fails if the goalie makes the save.

Don't be afraid to fail. If you are in the shooting zone, shoot. Simple as that. Make the goalie beat you. Don't beat yourself by not shooting, and don't change your style because the goalie makes a great save.

Even when the goalie makes the save, good things happen when you put the puck on the net. The puck might go in off a skate. You never know. So take the chance.

S E C

RETS

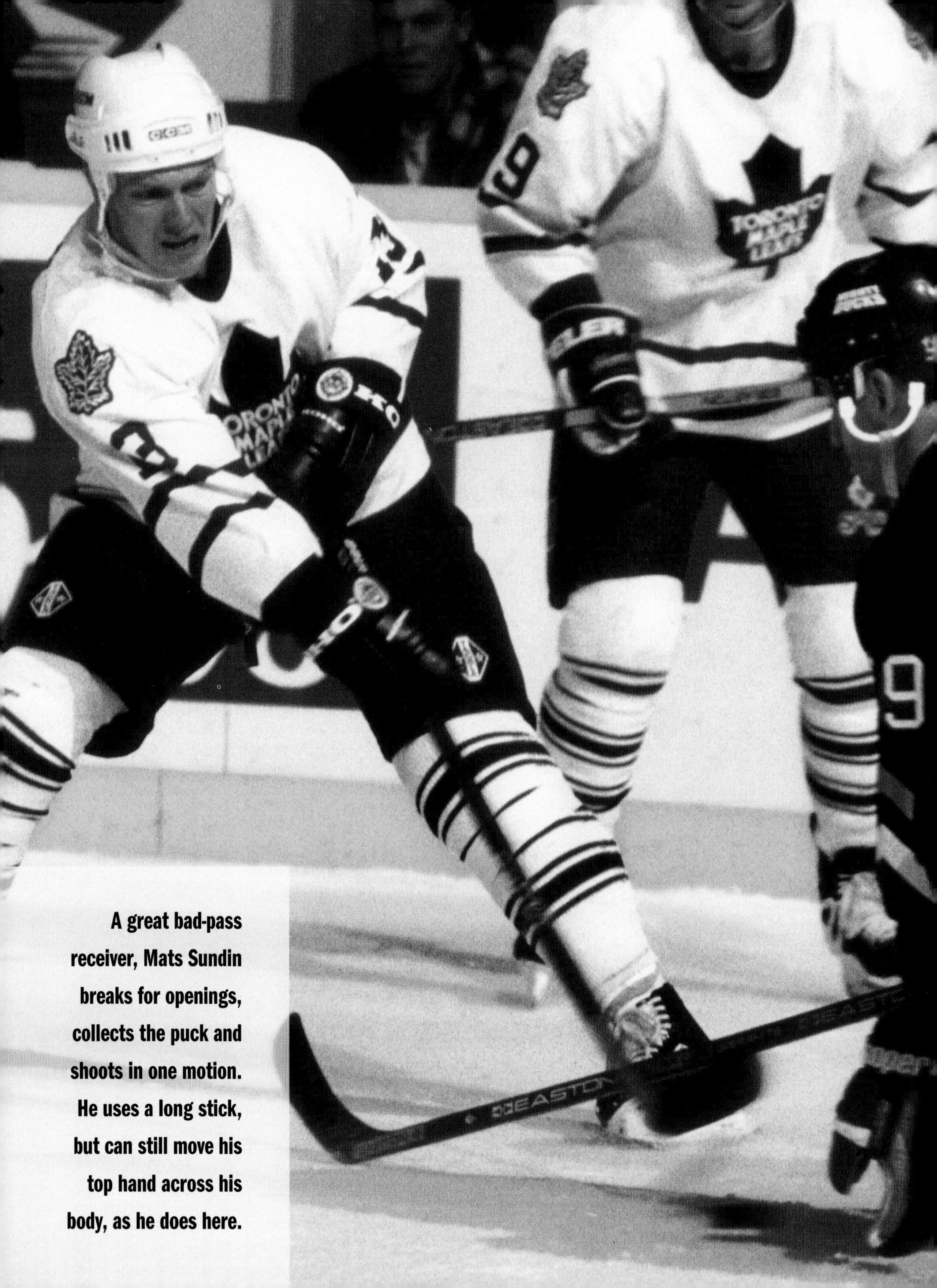

A great bad-pass
receiver, Mats Sundin
breaks for openings,
collects the puck and
shoots in one motion.
He uses a long stick,
but can still move his
top hand across his
body, as he does here.

Why do many hockey players wind up, hammer the puck and then usually miss the net? Good question. Maybe they like the noise the puck makes when it hits the glass. Or maybe it's because only great goal scorers follow these six rules—all the time.

1. Be ready

If you are anywhere near the net, carry the puck in the shooting or ready position. Your first option is always to shoot, so carry the puck to the net in the ready position. Then you can shoot at any time, off either foot.

2. Shoot quick

Shooting quickly is more important than shooting hard. It's not the fastest shot that scores—if the goalie is ready to stop it.

N H L T I P

"My most effective way to score is to use my speed and anticipation to get into openings and then release the puck as quickly as I can on net."

P A U L K A R I Y A

Always carry the puck in the shooting position if you're anywhere near the net.

Don't wait while you decide where to shoot. Scorers shoot quickly . . .

. . . and they get the puck on the net. You never know, it might go in.

Scoring secrets

But a quick shot takes the goalie by surprise, as Jason Arnott can tell you. "You have to get your shot off quickly because goalies are so good in the NHL, and, often, a quick shot is more successful."

3. Shoot on the net

Why would you do anything else? Simple. Some players only want to score on the perfect shot: top shelf, both posts and in, off the scoreboard, nothing but net. But you don't get points for style in this game. Make it easy on yourself. Hit the net.

4. Shoot low

Shoot low, unless you are in close and the goalie is down. A goalie's hands are quicker than his or her feet. Low shots produce more rebounds. Patrick Roy knows most of the goals scored against him come along the ice. That's why so many goalies play the butterfly style. But a butterfly goalie has to get down and back up. Any time you can catch the goalie moving—up or down on the ice, in or out of the net—shoot low.

5. Know the goaltender's weaknesses

Look for openings and shoot where you see the net. Look five-hole, then low stick-side. Goalies will tell you how to score on them—if you watch. Does the stick come off the ice when the

Scoring secrets

Shoot low. Brandon is moving sideways, opening the five-hole, but Jordan crosses in front and scores on the goalie's stick side.

Think save and expect rebounds. Pull the puck back and go upstairs.

goalie moves sideways? Is the glove hand high or low? Do you see a five-hole? How does the goalie handle being scored on? Those are some of the ways goalies tell you what to do.

6. Expect rebounds

Be at the net when your teammates shoot and have your stickblade on the ice. Let's face it: not all of your team's shots are going to go in. Go where you think the puck will be after the goalie makes the save. If it goes in, what did you lose? If not, make the second shot count. Or the third.

"My favourite move is when the puck goes over the line. You don't think. You just react. Is the goalie on the goal line or out? I look at the goalie and it just happens."

PAVEL BURE

Learning doesn't make you smart. It makes you educated. Developing hockey skills doesn't always make you a star, either, but it will make you a better hockey player. And it will teach you that you can learn with your body, just as you learn with your mind.

You already do many things without thinking. Spelling common words, for example, or doing simple math problems in your head. It's the same with hockey. Skills that are awkward at first become smooth and effortless if you do them often enough.

This chapter can help you become better with the puck. And once you stop thinking about stick-handling and deking, you can think about other things—like what you'll do when you get to the net.

STICK

SKILLS

If you can't receive the puck, and carry and protect it from your opponents, you can't play hockey. Luckily, good stickhandlers are not born, they're made. You can make yourself a magician with the puck. All you need to do is practise the tips and drills in this section.

Check your stick

Usually, the first step you can take to improve your stickhandling is to shorten your stick. Your stick is your main tool for handling the puck. In order to make a tight turn away from your shooting side, you need to be able to move your top hand across in front of your body with your stickblade flat on the ice. Is your stick short enough to do that?

Stickhandling

Tyler shows proper puck-carrying stance: knees flexed, hands relaxed, head up.

Gloves off, we can see him grip the stick with his fingers, not his palms.

You get a better feel by cupping the puck with the toe of your stick.

T I P

Practise stickhandling without your gloves, so you can see yourself using your wrists.

In good hands

A good stickhandler uses a short grip, with hands close together (8–12 inches/20–30 cm apart) at the top of the stick.

Roll your wrists to handle the puck. One way to make sure you use your wrists is to keep your elbows away from your body. Don't squeeze your stick. Use an easy grip, mostly with your fingers.

You can control the puck best with the middle-to-toe areas of your stickblade. That's where your wrist movements have the greatest effect. That's where you have the most feel.

Practising stickhandling drills will turn you into a smooth, tricky, puck-control artist. The drills in this section were developed by Dave King, an NHL and Canadian National Team coach. They can be done at the rink or on any other smooth surface.

Practise on your own

■ Stand with one foot on each side of a line. Focus on using your wrists, and make quick, neat sweeps. Do narrow and wide sweeps. Do the same with only your top hand, then your bottom hand. Next, move the puck back and forth, but lift your stick 12 inches/30 cm or so between sweeps. Do narrow and wide sweeps, but always lift your stick. This drill will prepare you for handling the puck when your opponents' sticks are nearby.

Side to side across the line. Quick movements.

Jesse rolls his wrists and keeps his elbows out as he does figure-8s.

Weight shift from foot to foot, hands 12 inches/30 cm apart. Cup the puck.

Stickhandling drills

■ Add footwork. Place your gloves on the ice 3 feet/90 cm apart. Move the puck in a figure-8 around the gloves, both ways. Move your feet when you have to, but stay square to the gloves. After a few sessions, start moving your head: up, down, side to side. Use the toe of your blade.
■ Now set your gloves 6 feet/1.8 m apart. Move your feet so you go from side to side while doing a figure-8 with the puck. Use a T-push to move sideways. Remember: To make the forehand move, your top hand must cross in front of your body.

"I try to relax and not get worked up over any particular game. I try not to get too high when things are going well, or too low when things are going poorly."

STEVE YZERMAN

Practise with others

These drills will help you become more aware of your opponents as you stickhandle, help you avoid checks, and to begin making quick changes of direction with the puck. To practise these drills, you'll need at least six other players.

■ Each player takes a puck and stickhandles within a circle. The idea is to control your own puck while poke-checking everyone else's puck out of the circle. Remember: When your puck is under attack, get your body between the puck and the checker. Also, try moving your puck to an open area while poke-checking someone else's puck, then retrieve it.

■ Each player puts his or her bottom glove on the ice. When you come to a glove, make a sudden turn around the glove to your forehand or backhand.

Watch your head

Coaches often tell you to keep your head up when you're handling the puck, but it's very hard to do. You have to look down sometimes, look up a lot and look to both sides. The idea is to keep your head moving. Think of your head as being on a swivel. Try to feel the puck through your fingers.

Watch other players

Watch how other players handle the puck. Even in the NHL, most players handle the puck too much. That slows you down. Some players move the puck from side to side even when there's no one near them. That's a waste of time. Remember: Keep the puck on your stick only when you have to protect it. Move the puck ahead of you to open ice, then go get it. That's the best way to beat a checker. It also means you're passing the puck to yourself, and passing is always the fastest way to move the puck.

Stickhandling drills

Stickhandling your way through an opposing team is one of the great thrills of hockey. It requires the ability to control the puck with your stick and skates, as well as a skill known as "deking."

Stickhandling is the way you handle the puck and carry it with you. The first thing you'll notice when you're handling the puck in a game is that you attract checkers. Deking is what you do to get past them.

There are many ways to deke. You can go from forehand to backhand, or vice versa. But all dekes have some kind of fake as part of the move, and work best when completed at full speed. In fact, just speeding up at the right time is a deke in itself.

The term "deke" comes from "decoy." A decoy is used to draw someone or something into a trap. *Your* bait is the puck. You hold it out to an opponent; when the checker goes for it, you take

Deking

Here the puck carrier dekes toward the boards, then moves the puck between the checker's stick and skates . . .

. . . then he bursts past, picking up the puck and skating hard.

it back and speed on past. The idea, of course, is to be tricky. Coach Dave King calls deking the most creative part of hockey.

One common type of deke is to move the puck through the triangle formed by an opponent's stickblade and toes, then move quickly to pick up the puck and skate around the checker. Add a head fake away from the direction you intend to go, then move the puck through the checker's stick and skates. The drills in this section focus on this type of deke.

A left-hand shot, 50-goal scorer Peter Bondra plays right wing, using his speed to create space, as he does here, cutting toward the net to shoot in midstride.

"Look at the holes
and not at the goalie.
Think shoot first.
If you see an opening,
that's when you can
deke, like when the
goalie's too far out."

PETER FORSBERG

You'll need at least six other players for these drills.

- The players form a circle. Each time you approach another player, make a fake one way, then move sideways in the other direction and accelerate as you pass by. Make the fake from more than a stick length away, or from out of poke-check range.

- All of the players put their bottom-hand gloves on the ice. You then fake one way and move sideways in the other direction. After a minute or so, put the top end of a stick into one of the gloves to show how far from the glove to make your move—a poke-check away.

- Half of the players stand with their stickblades on the ice as "dummy" checkers. The others sweep the puck back and forth between the sticks and feet of the checkers. Lift your stick over the checker's stick. Remember: Try to keep your stick movements quick and your elbows out. Roll your wrists. Puck carriers and checkers alternate.

- First, pick a player to be the "coach." The dummy checkers then stand astride the lines halfway across the rink, facing the puck carriers at the boards. Carry the puck to the dummy checker, make a move outside the checker's reach one way, move the other way, then accelerate past. The "coach" calls "Fake left, go right," or "Fake right, go left."

- Now attack the triangle. Move the puck between the dummy checker's stick and feet, move sideways, then pick up the loose puck and accelerate past.

- Pick a player to be the "coach." Now add a fake before moving the puck through the triangle. The "coach" calls "Fake right, go left," or "Fake left, go right." Speed past the checker when you regain the puck.

Deking drills

Passing is what makes hockey a team game. When you play as a team against six individuals who happen to be wearing the same jerseys, you win every time. Why? Because the right pass beats more than one checker. Two or three good passes will put the puck at your opponents' doorstep.

When you have the puck, remember: you have four teammates you can pass it to. When your team has the puck but you don't, your job is to get free for a pass.

Passing is one of the easiest skills to practise and improve at. Receiving passes is usually more difficult. So work on becoming a dependable receiver. If your teammates know you'll make the effort, you'll see a lot of the puck.

P A S

JOE SAKIC ▶

SING

There are four basic passes in hockey. In each case, make sure that you:

- keep both hands away from your body, so that your stickblade stays square to the target until the follow-through, and
- cup the puck with your stickblade.

    If you find your top hand is tight against your body, your stick may be too long or the lie may be incorrect.

The forehand pass

This is the easiest pass to make: a simple sweep of the stick toward the target. If your receiver is moving, remember to aim the puck well ahead of the receiver's stick, not their body. Bring the puck back to your back foot, release at the front foot. Follow through low, pointing your stickblade at the target.

Making passes

Jesse has his eye on his teammate, his stick cupping the puck . . . and his top hand away from his body. His hands work as a unit.

He follows through, shifting his weight and pointing his stick at the target.

The backhand pass

This pass is used when you want to get the puck to someone on your backhand side. Sight your target out of the corner of your eye. Try to keep your lower shoulder down, so your stickblade—and the puck—stay on the ice. Again, hands move together. The motion of a backhand pass causes your upper body to twist and your lower shoulder and hand to rise, making it easier to raise the puck. Follow through low. Stickblade square to the target.

The flip pass

To avoid sticks or bodies on the ice between you and your receiver, use a flip pass. Use your wrists to draw the puck toward yourself, and snap your stickblade up and under the puck. But don't overdo it. This is a pass, not a shot. Remember, the puck must land flat on the ice before it reaches the target.

The drop pass

This is the quickest way to move the puck between teammates, and often results in an unchecked puck carrier. The passer simply stops the puck and leaves it for the trailing teammate. But beware. Make sure that the player behind you is your teammate. If the player isn't, your opponents are off on a breakaway—and you are going in the wrong direction.

Upper hand away from the body, front shoulder down. Cup the puck.

Smooth follow-through. Weight on the front foot, point the stick at the target. Look where the pass is going.

Making passes

Passing checklist

- The right pass is usually the easy pass. The longer the pass, the less likely the puck will get there.
- Hands work together, not against each other. Keep your stickblade square to the target.
- If you are the puck carrier, try to make eye contact with your receiver. Many passes go untouched because the receiver has no idea they are coming.

A pass that is not received loses your team the puck most of the time. Count the number of passes tried, but not received, the next time you watch a game. Even in the NHL, too many players give up on passes that are not perfect.

Receiving passes is more difficult than making them. Practise receiving bad passes. Passes behind you, passes into your skates, passes coming from behind, passes that arrive in the air—all are chances to show how much you want the puck.

If the pass is off-target: Reach for the pass by dropping your bottom hand off your stick. This will extend your reach. Just stop the puck with your stick held by your top hand, then go after it.

If the pass is behind you: There are two things you can do. You can stop. Or you can reach back with your top hand on the stick and your stickblade angled so the puck will rebound up to your back skate. Kick the puck up to your stick, which you are now holding with both hands.

Receiving passes

Bad pass. Will lets go of the stick with his bottom hand and reaches with his top hand only. Front knee bends deep to give him better reach.

The puck will deflect ahead off Will's back skateblade to his stick.

T I P

To improve your pass receiving, get your elbows up as the puck gets close. This helps you get your entire stickblade on the ice.

If the pass is into your skates: Angle your skate on the side the pass is coming from, toe in, and deflect the puck up to your stick. Or, if the pass is coming further back, put one foot behind the other, creating a 2-foot/61-cm-long target for the puck to hit. Shorten up on your stick to control the puck better when it arrives.

If the pass is off the ice: Try to catch the pass without closing your hand on the puck. Just stop the puck with your open palm, drop it in front of you, and play the puck with both hands on your stick. Don't wave your stick at high passes.

Pass receiving checklist

- The trick to receiving passes is to be available. When your team has the puck, look for open ice.
- Think "catching," not "stopping," the puck when you receive a pass. Relax your grip. Reach toward the puck and absorb its impact.
- Part of being available for a pass is making it easy for the passer. Be visible. Try to skate across the passer's field of vision in the neutral zone. Hold your stick on the ice as a target.
- Sometimes the long way around is the shortest route to receiving the puck. By skating in a semicircle to a spot not

N H L T I P
"The key to receiving a bad pass is to use your entire body. Practise taking pucks off your skates and using your stick to knock down passes in the air."
P A U L   K A R I Y A

Jordan reaches back for a pass behind him. His stick deflects the puck toward him . . .

. . . and he kicks it up with his back foot . . .

. . . to his stickblade, angled inward to receive the puck. This requires practise.

Receiving passes

far away, you can be at full speed when the puck comes, and be better able to see it coming.
- Receive a bouncing puck with your skate behind your stick-blade. Don't lift your stick off the ice. Back it up with your foot.
- Don't give up on bad passes. The more often you convert bad passes to completed passes, the more you'll get the puck.

Canadiens captain Vincent Damphousse executes a textbook saucer pass—just over the checker's stick—that will land flat on the ice, on the tape of Valeri Bure's stick.

Most of the team drills in hockey involve passing. Here are a few simple drills that focus on this skill alone.

Playing catch

Two players face each other, 10–15 feet/3–4.5 m apart. Concentrate on keeping your hands and elbows away from your body. Make smooth, accurate passes, and follow through with your stickblade square to the target. Release the puck off the toe of the stick in a heel-to-toe action. The receiver reaches a few inches/centimetres toward the incoming pass. Lay a stick between the two players and practise flip passes.

Circle drill

Five or six players stand around the rim of a circle. Put your sticks on the ice and to the side as targets. The idea is to make smooth, accurate passes that hit the receiver's stick.

Pig-in-a-poke

Same as above, with one player, or "pig," in the middle trying to intercept. With skilled passers, add another "pig," then another puck. Players who have their passes intercepted or deflected move into the middle.

Skating & passing

Two players skate side by side, passing back and forth. The receiver stickhandles once or twice before returning the pass. Concentrate on leading the receiver with each pass.

Passing drills

The difference between scorers and everybody else is not skill level. The difference is that top scorers *think* differently. They know they can score. They know they can score from anywhere near the net. They know that even if the goalie makes the save there will be a rebound, and they go after that rebound.

Great scorers know that if they don't score this time, they will the next time. And you know what? So can you. Any decent hockey player can be a goal scorer. It helps to be able to receive, carry and protect the puck—these are the basic skills, and some goal scorers don't have them all. But the skill you need most, if you want to score goals, is the ability to shoot the puck accurately. This chapter shows you how.

S H O

TONY AMONTE▸

OTING

The wrist shot is an all-purpose, hard, accurate shot. It can be used when you are standing still or skating fast.

How to do it

Body position: Try to stay relaxed. Cup the puck with the middle of your stickblade. Feel it there. Keep your eyes on the target.

The shot: Sweep your stick forward. Just as it passes your body, bend both wrists back. Then snap them closed. The upper wrist pulls back on the top of your stick. The lower wrist supplies power and determines how high the shot will go.

Follow-through: Shift your weight to your front skate and follow through, aiming your stickblade at the target. To keep your shot low, follow through with your lower wrist on top of your stick and the toe of your stick pointing at your target.

The wrist shot

A textbook wrist shot starts with the puck well back . . .

. . . Jesse's power stroke is bending his stick as he lets the shot go . . .

. . . and follows through, pointing his stickblade at the target and rolling his bottom wrist over.

Wrist shot checklist

- Use both wrists. Turn both wrists open, and snap both closed at the moment of release. Feel your upper thumb pull the top of your stick toward your body.
- Shift weight from your back to front skate for power.
- Turn your body into the shot.
- Follow through, pointing your stickblade at your target, at the height you want. Feel your lower thumb curl around your stick to keep the shot low.

The closest thing to a secret weapon in hockey is the backhand shot. Vincent Damphousse uses it. Adam Oates uses a straight, shortened stickblade to improve his. And Mark Messier uses it more than any player in the NHL. Curved sticks have almost eliminated the backhand shot from the game, so goalies don't expect it. The backhand motion tells goalies to expect the puck to go high. Shooters who can keep their backhand shots down can score a lot of goals.

How to do it

The backhand shot is done exactly the same as the wrist shot, but from the other side of your body. Use the same sweeping motion with your stick, the same wrist snap, the same weight transfer from skate to skate and the same follow-through.

Jordan sneaks a peek at his target from the corner of his eye.

Power comes from upper body uncoiling and weight shift.

Keep it smooth. Keep the shot low by following through low.

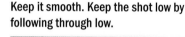

The backhand shot

Body position: Concentrate on dropping your front shoulder to get the stickblade flat on the ice.

Follow-through: A low follow-through keeps your backhand low.

Backhand checklist

- Just do it. Half the battle is trying the backhand shot.
- Get your body into it. Start with your front (lower) shoulder down. Keep your upper hand in close.
- Don't flip the puck. Drive it. Follow through low.

Quick rather than fast, shifty and a good stickhandler, Zigmund Palffy burst into the NHL with 43- and 48-goal seasons when he started shooting more and passing less.

The snap shot is the quickest shot you can get away, and it's one of the toughest shots for a goalie to stop. You can also shoot from close to your feet, so there is almost no windup, and no warning. It is a combination wrist and slap shot.

A crisp snap shot gives you the element of surprise—by enabling you to shoot from a crowd. It is tough to master, but very rewarding.

How to do it

The snap shot takes more practise than other shots. Work on shooting off all the points along a tight quarter-circle, running from your forehand side next to your front foot to right in front of your feet, with your front foot pointed out. Breathe out hard on the power stroke to add explosiveness.

Body position: The puck can be anywhere on your forehand side, even in front of you. You can be moving sideways across the goalmouth. It's also a great one-timer shot off a pass.

> **T I P**
> Bend your knees on the follow-through to keep your balance.

Michelle's weight is on her inside leg all the way.

The shot is released in front of the feet, before the goalie is ready.

Her body twists to add power. This is a classic snap shot.

The snap shot

Hands: Bring your stickblade back on the ice. Keep your wrists cocked on the power stroke, and your follow-through short. Contact point: middle of the blade. Stroke: short, but explosive.

Follow-through: Keep your balance; many players fall backward after the forward weight transfer. The rear foot often leaves the ice during the follow-through, so be aware of checkers nearby.

How to do it

You should wait to work on your slap shot. It is hard on you, hard on your stick and hard to control, and the windup takes time. But who wants to wait? What a feeling you get! What power! What a noise! If you're going to practise it, you might as well do it right.

Body position: The puck is opposite your front foot. Look at the puck, not the target. Keep your head down all the way.

Hands: Grip your stick firmly with your top hand. Slide your lower hand down the shaft as you reach back, then lock that hand.

The shot: Your weight will shift naturally to your front foot as you swing. Feel the entire force of your arms and shoulders behind the shot as your weight moves forward. Your stickblade should hit the ice just behind the puck, which you want to hit near the heel. Snap your wrists at the moment of impact.

The slap shot

Eyes on the puck. Breathe in. Keep your backswing low to get the shot off faster.

Get your body into it. Contact the ice a couple of inches behind the puck.

Continue the body twist. All weight on your front skate. Aim at the target.

Follow-through: Follow through as far as you want. Keep all your weight on your front foot as you swing your stickblade at the target. How high a slap shot goes depends on where in your swing you hit the puck—the further forward you hit it, the higher it will go.

Slap shot checklist

- Where is the puck? Look.
- Keep your head down until you follow through.
- Hit the ice a few inches/centimetres behind the puck.

"I'm always ready to shoot. The more you wait, the less of a chance you're gonna get. I'm looking for open net. If you're in close, you've got to pick the corner."

ALEX MOGILNY

John LeClair uses his size to get in close, and often shoots without looking, just to get the puck on the net. He has worked hard to improve his release.

Most goals are scored from within the "shooting zone"—an imaginary triangle on the ice from which most of the goalmouth can be seen. From here, you are close enough to the goal to beat the goalie with a good shot.

If you are in your opponents' shooting zone, you should almost always shoot the puck. Why not pass? Because the shooting zone is a busy place. A pass in the zone usually ends up on an opponent's stick, or sometimes your teammate will lose the puck. Pass *into* the shooting zone, but not from *inside* it.

The passing moment

The one time you *should* pass in the shooting zone is on a two-on-one—*if* you are 100 per cent sure you can get the puck past the defender. But always move the puck hard to the net and

N H L   T I P

"Read the play and select the best time to get into position for a shot from the slot. Know where and how your linemates react in certain scoring situations."
B R E T T   H U L L

If you have the puck inside this triangle, shoot. Your teammate takes the rebound.

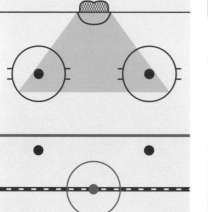

Here, Will's teammate, Tyler, is outside the shooting zone. *Never* pass from the slot. Tyler should go to the net.

The shooting zone

look as if you mean to shoot. Carry the puck in the ready position—on your shooting side. That's how to make the goalie commit to you, leaving your teammate for the easy tap-in.

Remember: If you have the puck in the shooting zone, you have a good chance to score. If you lose the puck, you lose that chance. Passing inside the shooting zone often loses the puck for your team. So shoot. Put the puck on the net. Then go to the net. Think rebound.

Look for weaknesses

Goalies have weaknesses. Do you know what they are? Take a moment to look at the opposing goalie during warmups. Note any habits that seem unusual. Above all else, check the goalie's stance, or ready position. Is the stickblade flat on the ice? Where is the catching mitt—too high? Too low? Does the goalie's stick come off the ice when he or she moves sideways?

Remember, there are two styles of goaltending: stand-up and butterfly. Each style has different strengths and weaknesses.

Stand-up

Stand-up goalies stay on their feet more of the time, and their leg pads are closer together. As you can see from the tips below, most of the time you need to shoot low against a stand-up goalie.

Study the goalie

A stand-up goalie is ready for high shots, so shoot for the lower corners.

Get the goalie moving sideways. Look high glove-side or low stick-side. Stay in front and think rebound.

T I P

If you can get a stand-up goalie to make a stick save, chances are there will be a rebound.

Stand-up checklist

- If the goalie is playing the angles just right, shoot low, on the open side.
- Is the goalie's stickblade flat on the ice? Covering the entire area between the goalie's feet? If not, shoot there.
- Is the goalie back in the net? Yes? Then shoot for the bottom corners.
- If the goalie's catching mitt is on your forehand side, and you can see net above it, go there.

Butterfly

Goalies usually adopt the butterfly style because of one important fact: more than two-thirds of all goals are scored into the bottom 12 inches/30 cm of the net. The idea behind the butterfly style is to get as much equipment as possible down into that 12 inches/ 30 cm. A butterfly goalie trades goals through the five-hole for saves on shots to the lower corners. Your mission is to take advantage of that trade.

Butterfly checklist

- Shoot first. Butterfly goalies tend to play back in the net, which creates openings.
- Look at the five-hole first. How fast does the goalie move up and down? Catch the goalie moving, if you can.

> **T I P**
> Most goals scored on butterfly goalies are made at ice level, as the goalie is going down.

If you can catch a butterfly goalie going down, there will be three holes down low to shoot at. Look for them.

In the butterfly position, shoot over the 12-inch/30-cm width of the goalie's pads. A catcher moves up better than down.

Study the goalie

- It is almost impossible for a goalie to move up and down *and* keep a stickblade flat on the ice. Watch and see.
- A butterfly goalie's feet are wide apart in the ready position. The stickblade can't cover all that space. Look for the opening between the stickblade heel and the skate on that side.
- The first 12 inches/30 cm off the ice is also the legal width of a goalie's leg pads. Aim a little higher and just inside the post.
- Once a butterfly goalie is down, that goalie is unable to move sideways. So move sideways yourself, then shoot.

Finally. It's you and the goalie. You've imagined this moment dozens of times. What do you do? The goalie will tell you. Not by talking, but by showing you how he or she is playing. It's called "body language." It's not hard to figure out. All you have to do is look.

Is the goalie in or out of the net? Stand-up or butterfly? No matter how the goalie is playing, there are several options you can use. Read and react.

Scoring is a numbers game. Not the number of goals and assists you rack up, but the options you have each time you're in scoring position. There is always more than one way to score. It's your choice. See what the goalie is giving you, and take it.

Always remember: *You* have the puck. That gives you the edge.

S C O

RIN

When you are in the shooting position, you carry the puck to one side. That means the puck has a different view of the net and the goalie than you do. This is called the "shooter's illusion."

There are two differences between what you see and what the puck sees. First, the puck is on the ice while your eyes are well above it. Second, the puck is almost the length of your stick away from you. The difference between what you see and what the puck sees can work for or against you. You can make this illusion work for you.

In front

Say you are directly in front of the net, with the puck on your stick, forehand side. The goalie, too, is standing exactly in the middle of the goalmouth. You see the same amount of net on both sides of the goalie. But the puck sees more net than you do. So you shoot.

The shooter's illusion

The goalie is lined up with the shooter, not the puck. Go short side.

The goalie is playing her angle perfectly. There's very little to shoot at.

Coming from your proper wing, the puck sees more net on the short side.

On your wing

It works even better from an angle. Say you shoot left—most right-handers do—and you are on your proper wing, between the faceoff dot to the left of the net and the goal crease. The goalie, once again, is midway between the posts as you see them. But the puck sees more net on the short side. If you see net there, shoot to that side. Go for the rebound.

The off-wing

Here's where the shooter's illusion works best of all. You are on your off-wing, the right side. Same situation: goalie centred. The puck sees more net on the far, or long, side. And the closer you get to the net, the more net the puck sees. So get closer and shoot for the far side.

You won't see the opening, but the puck will. *You* might not even see it go into the net.

If the goalie is playing the angles right

Don't get fooled. Goalies learn about the shooter's illusion the hard way. A goalie playing the angles correctly lines up with the puck, not your body. When this happens, in the examples above you will see more net on the short side. But that is the same illusion working for the goalie. It's called "playing the angles."

T I P
Check whether the goalie is lined up with the puck *or* your body. If the goalie is centred between the posts, you have the edge. Take your best shot.

Here's one way the shooter's illusion can work for the goalie. You see lots of net up high . . .

. . . but the puck, down on the ice, sees very little net. Brandon has everything covered.

The shooter's illusion

Shooter's illusion checklist

- On a breakaway, start giving yourself the edge by moving a bit to one side or the other. Make the goalie react.
- If the goalie doesn't move, shoot the puck. Most of the time, you'll hit nothing but net.
- The closer you are to the net, the more net the puck will see. Move in closer.

Theoren Fleury has made himself a star in a bigger man's game with speed and intensity: his feet are always moving, and he shoots from anywhere near the net.

Call them garbage goals. That's because rebounds are the easiest way to score. All you do is shovel them into the net. In one survey of 1,200 NHL goals, close to half of them were scored from within 10 feet/3 m of the net. But you must want to score, because right in front of the net can be a painful place to be. Standing in front attracts a lot of attention.

What to do

1. Form a tripod with your skates and stick.
2. Lean on your stick. Be solid. Think save.
3. Know where the shot is coming from, then watch the goalie's pads. You can't react in time if you watch the shot, but watching the goalie's pads tells you where the rebound will go.
4. Time your arrival at the net. Drive for the net even when the goalie seems to have the puck.

> **T I P**
> High shots are usually caught and held. Low shots create rebounds. So shoot low.

The key to rebounding is to be where the puck will go. Here, a shot from the corner rebounds out front . . .

. . . where Nicolas, now free of his checker, has plenty of room to shoot for the far side.

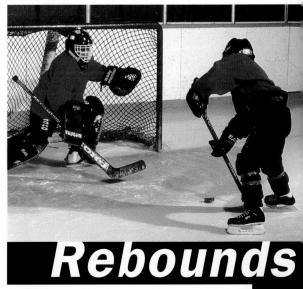

Rebounds

Rebound checklist

■ Don't be surprised when a rebound comes your way. Expect it.
■ Don't rush your shot. Take your time.
■ Use your body to protect the puck. Expect to get hit.
■ If a rebound is close to the goalie and the goalie is down, pull it back and shoot high.
■ Even when the net is open, shoot hard and try to get the puck off the ice.

Of any close-in play, crossing in front is the one that gives you the most chances to score. In fact, it's better than a breakaway. On a breakaway, you're in a big rush. You're being chased. But if you're crossing in front you take the defense by surprise. Often, you have all the time in the world.

You also have more chances to score when you cross in front. Think about it. On a breakaway you usually get one move, and that move depends on what the goalie is doing. When you cross in front, you make the goalie move sideways across 6 feet/ 1.8 m of goalmouth. That gives you more chances to score. The goalmouth is wide, the puck is small.

So when you find yourself alone with the puck in your opponents' corner, and your teammates are all covered, there is something you can do. Just walk out front—like you own the rink—and take your chances.

Crossing in front

Michelle holds the near post, so Jordan fakes the shot and goes across. Even when she makes the second save...

...the rebound gives Jordan a third scoring chance. He buries it.

TIP

Any time you can cross in front of the net you give yourself five chances to score—that's better than a breakaway.

What to do

You have five choices:

1. If the goalie guesses you mean to cross in front, he or she may leave the short-side post as you approach. Watch for this opening. Tuck the puck in the short side.
2. If you are coming from your proper wing, you may be able to break for the front of the net while trailing the puck behind you. When the goalie moves with you, go high to the short side.

3. The goalie cannot move across the net without stepping in the same direction. Fake the shot to hold the goalie at the post. Then, when the goalie opens the pads to go with you, tuck the puck in between.

4. If the goalie does a double-pad slide across the net, look back. The goalie's upper body will be the last thing to hit the ice. Slide the puck underneath.

5. If none of these openings were there, the goalie is now flat on the ice. Carry the puck past the far post and throw it high.

Crossing-in-front checklist

- Watch out for the goalie's poke-check as you get close to the short side. Look for the stick hand to dart up the shaft of the goalie's stick. Be ready to shoot when the goalie lunges at you.

> ### N H L   T I P
> "When you go wide you can gain speed on the outside and then cross in front—it's been a successful move for me."
> **S E R G E I   F E D O R O V**

This time Jordan crosses from his proper (left) wing, fakes the shot to freeze the goalie . . .

. . . and keeps on going, giving himself an open net for a backhand or forehand shot.

Crossing in front

- Focus on the net and the goalie. Skate hard. Commit yourself. Aim to cross at the edge of the crease.
- Look short side first.
- Next, wait for the goalie's feet to turn and open. Don't shoot the puck between the goalie's legs, just tap or deflect it in when you see the opening.
- Once you are across—if you haven't already scored yet—look for the backhand over or past the goalie's foot.

> "Speed is the key for me. If I don't have my speed I'm not going to have many chances. Speed, timing and reading the play—those are the keys to scoring chances."
>
> **TEEMU SELANNE**

Sometimes it comes down to just you and the goalie—one play for all the marbles. When this happens, all you need to do is focus on one thought: *you* have the upper hand. After all, the puck is on your stick. Remember: You decide what's going to happen, so have a plan.

And relax. You know what you're going to do. The goalie doesn't.

What to do

On a breakaway, there are lots of ways to score. But the move you choose will depend on the goalie's position. Memorize the following breakaway moves, and practise them in your mind and on the ice. Before you make your move, check three things: Is the goalie in or out? Is the goalie playing the angle right? Is the goalie moving sideways?

Breakaways

Kendall is perfectly positioned—there's not much here to shoot at.

So Will moves right to give himself an angle . . .

. . . and goes to his backhand to make the most of it.

Is the goalie in or out?

Goalie in = shot: If the goalie is back in the net, carry the puck in front to fake the deke, then shoot for the net you can see. Move to your forehand side a bit to improve your angle.

Goalie out = deke: If the goalie is out of the net, cutting off the angle, you need to fake the shot, then go around to your forehand side.

Goalie moves first = shoot for opening: Some goalies will guess, and make the first move. Go the other way.

Is the goalie playing the angle right?

Is the goalie playing the angle right, taking away the shot and moving backward to take away the deke? That's what the goalie *should* be doing. Both of you are moving toward the net. The goalie has the advantage.

Make the goalie move: Step sideways. Fake one way, then go the other way. No goalie can go two ways at once.

Is the goalie moving sideways?

Once you have the goalie moving sideways, you have more options. The openings to look for are a lot like the ones you see when you cross in front of the net.

Goalie moving sideways = between feet: Watch for the goalie's legs to open. Tap the puck in between.

Get the goalie moving sideways, and you have an edge.

By going to his backhand, Tyler changes the angle by 4 feet/1.2 m.

The goalie is down and the net is open. Tyler should score.

Breakaways

Breakaway checklist

- Prepare for breakaways. Expect them.
- Read and react. Let the goalie tell you what to do.
- Carry the puck in the shooting position.
- If you can—say, on a penalty shot—set up an angle at the blue-line. For example: Turning a bit to your backhand side sets up the off-wing angle at the net. That's the Mario Lemieux way.
- Know which side of the goalie your forehand shot will attack. *Stick side:* shoot low. *Glove side:* shoot high.

"A long reach gives you the ability to move the puck from one side of the crease to the other. The further you can move the puck, the further the goalie has to go to stop it."

ERIC LINDROS

Go to the net

More than half of all goals scored in the National Hockey League come from within 10 feet/3 m of the net; many of those are scored from the edge of the crease. Keith Tkachuk, for example, scores most of his 50+ goals a year from close in.

Playing chicken

A good goalie waits for your move. A good scorer makes the goalie move. How far? Going from your forehand to your backhand is like moving the puck from post to post. It's a good move, but it's the most common deke. Going from your backhand to your forehand—the way Eric Lindros does—is a *great* move. Work on it.

Be prepared

Skill-testing question: What is the difference between a bad pass and a good pass? Answer: The receiver. You can't score without the puck, and the best way to get it is to reach for it when it comes your way. Just watch how Joe Sakic does it.

Speed kills

Teemu Selanne and Peter Forsberg are proof that your feet can be scoring weapons. The faster you can skate, the more opportunities you will get.

Get creative

Good scorers can score from anywhere. If the goalie is not tight against the post, put the puck in off his or her body.

Know the goalie

If you shoot *right* and the goalie is right-handed, your first option is over the catcher. If you shoot *left* and the goalie is right-handed—the most common matchup—shoot low stick-side.

Adding it up

Resources

Videos

Puck Control and Deking

International Hockey Centre of Excellence, with Dave King.
Stickhandling, puck control and deking skills broken down into
a series of simple drills that can make any player an offensive
threat.

Skate Shoot Score

By Stuart Davison. 55 min., Top Drawer Productions, 1988.
Equipment, warmup exercises, skating fundamentals,
stickhandling drills, shooting.

The Shooter's Edge

*Featuring Geoff and Russ Courtnall, with instructors Jim Park
and Scott Howson. 57 min., Snapshot Productions, 1991.*
Based on their analysis of 1,200 NHL goals, the instructors
show where, when and how to score in almost every offensive
situation. Well organized, well produced.

Wayne Gretzky's Hockey Tips

National Hockey League Players' Association, 1994.
The Great One, with Pavel Bure, Sergei Fedorov, Trevor Linden,
Marty McSorley and others, demonstrates skills. Includes
clips from NHL action, as well as rollerblading basics.

Brendan Shanahan, who believes young players should play all positions, is at his best right at the net. Coming from his off-wing, with either side of the net to shoot at, he is a fearsome sight for goaltenders.

Photo credits

Photography by Stefan Schulhof/Schulhof Photography, except as indicated below:

Photos by Bruce Bennett Studios:
Front cover: Tony Biegun
Back cover & title page spread (Keith Tkachuk, Paul Kariya, Mark Messier), p. 1 (background), p. 4, p. 7, p. 14 (background), p. 15, p. 30, p. 40, p. 44 (background), p. 45, p. 48: Bruce Bennett
Back cover & title page spread (Joe Sakic, Tony Amonte), p. 24 (background), p. 25, p. 32 (background), p. 33, pp. 52–53, p. 56: John Giamundo
Back cover & title page spread (Jaromir Jagr), p. 8 (background), p. 9, p. 21, p. 22: Richard Lewis
p. 18: Tony Biegun
p. 36: Jim McIsaac
p. 59: Layne Murdoch

Photo by Doug MacLellan/Hockey Hall of Fame: p. 10

Photos by Kallberg/Darch Studio: p. 13, p. 39

Photo of Brian Burke on p. 5 courtesy of the NHL